The Library of
Political Assassinations

The Assassination of
William McKinley

Antoine Wilson

The Rosen Publishing Group, Inc.
New York

This is to Irving 'n' Ellen Cohen.

Published in 2002 by The Rosen Publishing Group, Inc.
29 East 21st Street, New York, NY 10010

Library of Congress Cataloging-in-Publication Data

Wilson, Antoine.
The assassination of William McKinley / Antoine Wilson. — 1st ed.
p. cm. — (The library of political assassinations)
Includes bibliographical references and index.
Summary: Discusses the assassination of the twenty-fifth president, showing the political situation at the time as well as McKinley's legacy.
ISBN 0-8239-3546-9 (library binding)
1. McKinley, William, 1843–1901—Assassination—Juvenile literature.
2. McKinley, William, 1843–1901—Assassination. [1. Presidents.]
I. Title. II. Series.
E711.9 .W55 2001
973.8'8'092—dc21

2001002349

Manufactured in the United States of America

(Previous page) President William McKinley, the twenty-fifth president of the United States, served from 1897 to 1901, when he was killed by an assassin.

Contents

This column at Antietam National Battlefield in Sharpsburg, Maryland, honors President William McKinley.

Introduction

About a hundred years ago, on September 6, 1901, a man named Leon Czolgosz (pronounced chol-gosh) shot President William McKinley at the Pan-American Exposition in Buffalo, New York. McKinley died eight days later. Czolgosz rationalized the shooting by saying that it was his duty to help the working people in the United States. Czolgosz believed that by killing McKinley, he was helping to further a movement called anarchism. Anarchists believe the government is unnecessary and feel strongly that governments and rulers should be dismantled and that people should be able to live in total freedom. (The word "anarchy" comes from the Greek word *anarkhos*, which means "without a chief.") Czolgosz was concerned that President McKinley held too much power and that regular Americans did not have enough.

Czolgosz's beliefs, however extreme they may have seemed, were partly a response to what was going on in the country at the time. As president, McKinley had begun to expand the powers of his office, as well as increase the status of the United States as an influential world power. Decisions that were made in Washington, D.C., were affecting people all over the world. For example, during the Spanish-American War, McKinley was able to telegraph orders from the United States and have them followed in faraway places like Cuba and the Philippines. Some Americans believed that the United States should not meddle in the business of foreign countries. These people were deeply concerned about the president's increasing power. Many of McKinley's detractors gave speeches and published newsletters about anarchy and other radical political ideas. This was where Czolgosz picked up some of his anarchist notions.

As it turned out, killing McKinley did little to advance the aims of the anarchists. As a matter of fact, it hurt them. First of all, because President McKinley had been a popular president and was widely known as a kind and gentle man, the American public became fiercely antianarchist. Second, the assassination resulted in the swearing in of Vice President Theodore Roosevelt to the office of the president, and Roosevelt believed that McKinley had not taken big enough steps toward giving the presidency more authority. Although the anarchists claimed that Czolgosz had nothing to do with their movement, the label stuck, and even today Czolgosz is known as the "deranged anarchist" who took the life of the twenty-fifth president of the United States.

An Appointment with Death

Friday, September 6, 1901, was a day of great excitement at the Pan-American Exposition in Buffalo, New York. The day before had been President's Day at the exposition, and before an estimated crowd of 50,000 people, President William McKinley had given what some said was the best speech of his life. On that Friday, the president was welcomed to the exposition as a guest, and he had arranged a reception for the thousands of citizens who wanted to meet him and shake his hand. This was not unusual for the president, who had in fact made several train trips around the country, stopping in small towns to greet and talk with regular Americans.

A Security Risk?

What is noteworthy is that regardless of Secretary to the President George B. Cortelyou's concern about the security risks of the public reception, McKinley insisted on receiving people face-to-face. After all, he was the people's president—their elected representative—and his popularity was on an upswing. McKinley

President William McKinley speaks at the Pan-American Exposition in Buffalo, New York, on September 6, 1901. He was shot later that day.

had just brought America out of an economic recession and he had led the country to victory in the Spanish-American War. McKinley thought Cortelyou was being too cautious. "Why should anyone want to harm me?" he had asked.

The People's President: The Scarlet Carnation

The reception was scheduled for 4 PM at the Temple of Music on the exposition grounds. It was an unbearably hot day, and the area was very crowded. Twenty thousand people had gathered in and around the building to see the president. McKinley arrived just before 4 PM, and shouts of welcome erupted through the crowd. An organ played patriotic music while the president entered the building. The reception area was set up so that the president stood between Secret Service agents (the men who protect the president) and in front of some potted palm trees. Directly above and behind McKinley hung a giant American flag. As president, he prepared to meet the public; he took a moment to make sure he looked sharp in spite of a long hot day of traveling.

Excerpts from McKinley's Last Speech

On the United States economy:

"My fellow citizens, trade statistics indicate that this country is in a state of unexampled prosperity."

On trade policies with other countries:

"Only a broad and enlightened policy will keep what we have."

"What we produce beyond our domestic consumption must have a vent abroad."

On the rise of the United States as a global power:

"The period of exclusiveness is past. The expansion of our trade and commerce is the pressing problem."

On the necessity of a canal across Central America:

"We must build the Isthmian canal, which will unite the two oceans and give a straight line of water communication with the western coasts of Central America, South America, and Mexico."

Temple of Music, where Pres. McKinley, was shot, Buffalo, N. Y.

This postcard of the ornate Temple of Music in Buffalo, New York, commemorates the assassination of President McKinley. William McKinley is featured in the cameo on the left, and his wife, Ida, is in the one on the right.

The doors opened at 4 PM, right on time. Cortelyou wanted to limit the reception to ten minutes, but because so many people had shown up, McKinley was prepared to go longer. Though exhausted from his busy schedule, the heat, and the fact that he had not eaten much, the president greeted people cheerily. He shook hands with everyone who came up to him. People shook the president's hand, exchanged a few words, and moved along. Everyone was very excited to meet McKinley. A little girl asked for the scarlet carnation he was wearing in his buttonhole. McKinley removed the carnation—his good luck charm—and pinned it to the girl's shirt.

The Secret Service at Work

Meanwhile, Cortelyou and the Secret Service agents were keeping a close eye on the people waiting to meet the president. They noticed a suspicious looking young man—a little wild looking—hunched over, approaching in the line. They kept a keen watch over this man because they were concerned that he might try to harm McKinley.

When the man got to the front of the line, he looked at McKinley oddly and shook his hand, but would not let go. A Secret Service agent removed the man's hand from McKinley's, and then the man moved on. Security breathed a sigh of relief; nothing had happened.

The next man in line, a clean-cut, freshly shaven young man in a suit, had a bandage on his right hand. McKinley was about to extend his right hand when he saw the bandage. He quickly extended his left hand so that the man wouldn't have to shake with his injured hand. Little did he know what the bandage concealed: a loaded five-chamber .32-caliber revolver.

Leon Czolgosz: The Man Who Shot McKinley

Leon Czolgosz had come to the exposition with one goal in mind: to kill the president. This was not the first time he'd seen McKinley. He'd been at his speech the day before. Afterward, he had spent the night in a room above Novak's saloon in Buffalo, where he'd signed the register as John Doe. Even though Czolgosz had very little money, he ate a big meal that day, then went to the barbershop to get a shave. Maybe he wanted to look good for his big day, or maybe he just did not want to arouse suspicion.

That morning, he had gone to Niagara Falls for the president's appearance there, but he had arrived too late and ended up taking the first train back to Buffalo. No one knows why he went to Niagara Falls. Perhaps Czolgosz just wanted to see the president up close before shooting him later in the day.

Czolgosz was twenty-eight years old, five feet seven and a half, and weighed 140 pounds. On September 6, he wore a gray suit and gave the impression of being a clean-cut young man who was eager to meet the president. He had large, deep-set blue eyes, slightly wavy brown hair, and full lips. Before arriving at the Temple of Music, he removed a revolver from his pocket, held it in his right hand, and quickly wrapped it up with a handkerchief—an action he had been practicing for a long time. With the gun wrapped

LEON CZOLGOSZ, WHO SHOT PRESIDENT McKINLEY.
The above pictures are snap-shots of the assassin taken just after his arrest.

This print from September 1901 contains four photographic portraits of Leon Czolgosz taken just after his arrest for the assassination of President McKinley.

In this painting, a horrified crowd looks on as Leon Czolgosz shoots President McKinley at the Pan-American Exposition in Buffalo, New York.

inside the handkerchief, it looked as though his right hand was bandaged. No one who saw Leon Czolgosz's bandaged hand suspected that he was hiding a gun.

Shots Fired in the Temple of Music

It was 4:07 PM. The instant McKinley's left hand touched Czolgosz's left hand, Czolgosz fired his gun. He shot through his handkerchief and at such close range that there were powder burns on McKinley's vest. Almost immediately, Czolgosz fired a second time. As McKinley started falling backward, security officers caught him and sat him down in a chair.

Ida Saxton McKinley:
First Lady of the United States

Ida Saxton was a cashier in her father's bank
when she began seeing William McKinley, the
local county prosecutor, in 1870. (They had met
two years earlier at a picnic, but it was some time
before they began courting.) This went on for
several months, and they were married in 1871.
Although Ida was known for her independence, a
series of tragedies starting in 1873 transformed
her. Both her mother and the McKinleys' second
child, Ida, died within a short period of time. The
child was less than five months old. Two years
later, their first child, Katie, succumbed to typhoid
fever, leaving the McKinleys childless. Weighed
down by these tragedies, Ida became depressed
and sickly. She never recovered. Around the same
time, Ida began to suffer from seizures. A devoted
husband, William McKinley was always careful to
make sure that his wife was well taken care of.

Czolgosz had shot him twice in the chest. McKinley's face was white, but he was conscious. He asked Cortelyou, "Am I shot?" When Cortelyou told him that, yes, he had been shot, McKinley said, "My wife, be careful how you tell her—oh, be careful."

Capturing the Assassin

James Parker, an African American waiter at the Pan-American Exposition, had been ahead of Czolgosz in the line of those who wanted to meet the president. Czolgosz had just shaken hands with McKinley and was pausing to savor the moment when he fired the shots. Parker immediately turned and pounced on Czolgosz, pinning him to the ground. Two Secret Service officers joined Parker, and together, they held Czolgosz down.

The crowd, which had been enthusiastic and happy at the opportunity to see their president, grew worried and angry, and they crowded at the scene of the crime. Half of them wanted to make sure that McKinley was all right. The other half were already seeking revenge on Czolgosz. Some of the guards also wanted to rough up Czolgosz. In one report of the afternoon's events, a guard was about to run his bayonet (a knife attached to the end of a rifle) through Czolgosz's body, but McKinley said, "Go easy on him, boys." This statement was indicative of McKinley's personality. Even after having been shot, McKinley was forgiving and merciful.

Mayhem

Meanwhile, the crowd was screaming, "Lynch him!" Once Czolgosz was apprehended, Secret Service agents and James Parker took Czolgosz to a secluded room in the Temple of Music. Guards had to push their way through to keep the angered crowd at bay. In a room, Czolgosz was held down on a table while being questioned. He told the guards that his name was Neiman, a false name he'd used before. "I done my duty," Czolgosz told them. He also told them that he was an anarchist. (See chapter 3 for more information on the anarchist movement at the turn of the century.)

This is the electric ambulance that carried President McKinley from the Temple of Music to the hospital.

The Struggle to Save McKinley

An electric ambulance was summoned, and the president was taken in to an emergency hospital on the exposition grounds—a nine-minute ride. While surgeons

Timeline: McKinley's Life

January 29, 1843
William McKinley is born to William and Nancy McKinley in Niles, Ohio; he is the seventh in a family of nine children.

1860
McKinley works as a school-teacher in Poland, Ohio.

1861–1865
McKinley enlists as a private in the Ohio volunteer infantry for four years of service. He is commissioned as a brevet major by Abraham Lincoln for gallantry in various Civil War battles.

1866
McKinley enters law school in Albany, New York.

1867
McKinley is admitted to the Ohio Bar Association.

1869
McKinley is elected prosecuting attorney of Stark County, Ohio.

1873
The McKinleys' second daughter, Ida, is born; she dies five months later.

1875
The McKinleys' first daughter, Katherine, dies of typhoid fever.

1876
McKinley is elected to Congress for the first time. (He is reelected in 1878 and serves until 1890.)

1891
McKinley is elected governor of Ohio. (He is reelected in 1893.)

1896
McKinley is elected president of the United States. (He is reelected in 1900.)

September 6, 1901
McKinley is shot by assassin Leon Czolgosz in Buffalo, New York.

September 14, 1901
McKinley dies of infected gunshot wounds in Buffalo, New York.

were examining McKinley's wounds, Dr. Herman Mynter entered the room. McKinley was extraordinary at remembering people's names and faces, a useful skill for a politician. When Dr. Mynter walked into the room, McKinley recognized him immediately. Dr. Mynter had been among the thousands of people the president had met the day before. McKinley said, "Doctor, when I met you yesterday, I did not imagine that today I should have to ask a favor of you."

Three physicians operated on McKinley for an hour and a half in poor light and high heat. The first bullet was quickly discovered. It fell out of McKinley's clothes when he was undressed for surgery. The bullet had deflected off a button and entered the flesh above his breastbone, but it did not penetrate any further into McKinley's chest. The wound created by the second bullet would prove to be fatal. The second bullet had entered McKinley's belly, five inches below his nipple and an inch and a half to the left of the center of the abdomen. The bullet went all the way through his stomach. When the surgeons opened him up, they saw a small entry wound on the front of his stomach. When they turned the stomach around, however, the exit wound was big and ragged. They sewed up both stomach wounds and looked for the bullet but couldn't find it, even after an hour and twenty minutes in surgery. After the surgery, the president was moved from the Pan-American Exposition's hospital to the residence of John Milburn. Soon after, Mrs. McKinley was notified; she bore the shocking news with courage and strength.

In the meantime, Thomas Edison had heard that the doctors were having trouble finding the bullet. He telegraphed the doctors and offered the use of his X-ray machine (which was on display at the exposition) to try to find the bullet. However, the doctors turned down his offer. They did not want to move McKinley, who was resting at the Milburn home, because he seemed to be recovering well from the surgery.

This is a woodcut illustrating Thomas Edison's X-ray machine.

Soon, however, an infection set in. It quietly took root inside the walls of McKinley's stomach and in his pancreas. Even while it seemed as though he was recovering, the infection was quietly advancing. Some of the doctors tried to remain hopeful, but Dr. Roswell Park knew that things were turning for the worse. A week after the shooting, Dr. Park said, "It is useless, gentlemen. I think we ought to have a prayer."

President William McKinley died at 2:15 AM on Saturday, September 14, 1901, eight days after being shot. Biographers at the time reported that his last words were, "Good-bye all, good-bye. It is God's way. His will be done," and that he murmured the words to "Nearer my God to thee," a favorite hymn. His actual last words, however, were whispered, moments before he died, to Dr. Presley Rixley. "Oh, dear," McKinley said.

McKinley Expands the Presidency and the Country

International affairs dominated William McKinley's presidency. In fact, it was through McKinley's focus on American interests abroad that the presidency became a more powerful position, and that the United States became a world power, expanding its reach into the Caribbean and the Pacific. However, these changes were not well received by everyone, and in protest, some radical political movements were developed during this era. One such movement, the anarchists, captured the imagination of Leon Czolgosz, the man who shot the president. Before delving into the underpinnings of anarchy, let's look at how McKinley changed the presidency, ushering it into a modern age.

Remember the *Maine*

It was early 1898, and McKinley had been in office for just under a year. Tensions between Spain and her colony, Cuba, had captured the attention of the American public. The Cubans had established an independence movement. They wanted the Spanish to leave so that they could rule their own country. Spain did not want to give up its New World colony. American newspapers reported how cruel the Spanish were being to the Cubans, and the American public wanted to see the United States help the Cubans.

On January 25, 1898, the second-class battle-ship the USS *Maine* sailed into the Havana harbor in Cuba in broad daylight. The *Maine* wasn't the United States's biggest ship, but it was larger than any-thing else in the Havana harbor. With two smoke-stacks and two large masts, it weighed over 6,000 tons. The navy had built it at a cost of $3 million, a huge amount of money in the late

Rebel soldiers cook at their camp during the insurrection of 1896. Cuba gained independence after the Spanish-American War of 1898 but remained under the influence of the United States.

nineteenth century. As the *Maine* cruised into the harbor, everyone could see that the ship had been scrubbed and cleaned, and that the sailors were neatly dressed in their winter service blue; the navy wanted to make a good impression on their hosts.

The arrival of the *Maine* seemed peaceful enough, but trouble was brewing in Havana. The ship was there because McKinley was concerned about the safety of Americans in Cuba. Riots had broken out weeks earlier, and mobs of Spanish officers had attacked the offices of the Cuban-liberation newspaper. These Spanish officers wanted Cuba to remain under Spain's control. McKinley hoped that the presence of the *Maine* would provide a safe place for Americans to go in case more fighting broke out. McKinley was also trying to send a message to Spain; he wanted to let the Spanish know that the United States was watching and that no more abuse of the Cuban people would be tolerated.

The *Maine* sat in the harbor for three weeks without incident, but the situation was tense. Spain appeared to be preparing for more clashes with the Cubans, and the Spanish warned that any nation that interfered in the situation would be repelled by force. In other words, their conflict with the Cubans was none of the United States's business. A letter from the Spanish minister in Washington, Enrique Dupuy de Lôme, to a friend in Cuba was intercepted and published in an American newspaper. In the letter, Dupuy de Lôme called McKinley weak and said that he was hungry for the admiration of the crowd. After that insult, the United States's intervention in Cuba seemed almost unavoidable.

This painting depicts the explosion of the battleship USS *Maine* in the Havana harbor on February 15, 1898.

One Hot Night in Havana . . .

Then, on the night of February 15, 1898, an accident occurred that would alter the destinies of Spain and the United States. It was an overcast and hot night in Havana, and almost everyone on the *Maine* had settled into his bunk for the night. The bugler played taps, and the music echoed throughout the calm harbor. Suddenly, there was a noise like a rifle shot. A second later, the ship sounded like it was coming apart. The sound of metal tearing and crunching was deafening. The lights went out aboard the ship, and it tilted to one side. Smoke and fire filled the air. The *Maine* had blown up and was sinking into the Havana harbor.

At 1:30 AM on February 16, 1898, Secretary of the Navy John D. Long received the following dispatch: "*Maine* blown up and destroyed tonight at 9:40 PM." Some 266 American sailors were killed, and some eighty more were injured.

This political cartoon by Grant Hamilton depicts Spain as an apelike monster, one blood-dripping hand smearing the tombstones erected to the sailors of the *Maine* and the other clutching a knife.

The Press and Public Opinion

Even though no one knew what had caused the blast, and the governments of Spain and the United States urged that no one jump to conclusions, the press came up with their own theories. Two newspapers in particular, William Randolph Hearst's *New York Journal* and Joseph Pulitzer's *New York World*, were shameless about making up sensationalist stories in the race to sell more newspapers.

These newspapers had been publishing reports (not all of them true) urging the United States to get involved in Cuba. The explosion of the *Maine* further energized them in their efforts to push America into war. The *World* pointed fingers at Spain without any evidence: "The *Maine* Explosion Was Caused by a Bomb—Suspicion of a Torpedo," read a headline. The *Journal* was even worse: "The Warship *Maine* Was Split in Two by an Enemy's Secret Torpedo"; "The Whole Nation Thrills With War Fever"; and the famous slogan, "Remember the *Maine*! To Hell With Spain!"

Contrary to the newspapers' stories, recent studies indicate that the *Maine* blew up on its own, by accident. The *Maine* ran on coal, and the coal was stored in holds below deck. Experts suspect that the coal may have caught fire spontaneously and set off stores of gunpowder in other holds.

The Spanish-American War: "A Splendid Little War"

American ambassador to Great Britain John Milton Hoy described the Spanish-American War as a "splendid little war" because it was short and resulted in the United States's entrance into imperial politics. McKinley asked Congress for $50 million in national defense money and got it quickly. Among other things, he wanted to buy two Brazilian ships before Spain could. There were a limited number of fighting ships available in the world, so the United States and Spain scurried around trying to buy what they could. By buying the two brand-new Brazilian ships, McKinley showed the Spanish that the United States had the resources to equip itself for an all-out war and that the United States would pay big money to prevent available ships from becoming part of the Spanish fleet.

In March, a report came out that blamed Spain for the *Maine* explosion. The report was wrong, we now know, but at the time, the false accusation led to the possibility of war.

In April, McKinley addressed Congress. He described the situation with Spain and stated what could be done to avoid war. He said that if the United States did enter into war with Spain, it would be in the name of humanity—in order to free the Cubans. What is interesting is that he didn't simply ask Congress to declare war. Instead, he asked it to give him the power to end the conflict between Spain and Cuba, and to establish a new government in Cuba, "using American military forces as necessary."

Some saw McKinley as weak, since he did not ask for war outright. But McKinley's strategy was actually very clever: He was asking for discretionary power. In other words, he was asking for the right to act as he saw fit and to do so without having to ask Congress every time he wanted to take action. The political system of the United States is designed with a system of checks and balances. None of the three branches (executive, legislative, and judicial) can gain much power over the others. But McKinley was very cleverly expanding the powers of the executive branch, especially in terms of international affairs.

The Three Branches of the Federal Government

✪ **The legislative branch** includes Congress, which is made up of the House of Representatives and the Senate. These two groups have the power to propose and make laws.

✪ **The judicial branch** includes the Supreme Court. The Supreme Court explains and interprets the law based on the Constitution.

✪ **The executive branch** includes the office of the president. The president has the power to enforce laws and oversee the government. Thomas Jefferson and other Founding Fathers did not want a strong executive branch. They believed that a weak executive branch would keep government from abusing its power. (They were reacting, of course, to the English system, which had an extremely strong "executive branch" at the time: the king.) The United States was founded on a platform of decentralized power. Thomas Jefferson wrote, "I am not for transferring all the powers of the States to the General Government, and all those of that government to the executive branch." The executive branch gained significant power during McKinley's presidency.

Young men fighting in the Spanish-American War are seen above.

Finally, on April 25, McKinley asked Congress to declare war. The war itself was short (the United States won in three months), and American troops suffered more from unclean camp conditions than they did from battle. In addition to ousting the Spanish from Cuba, McKinley ordered that American forces attack Spanish forces in the Philippines, where another independence movement was raging against Spain.

Victory and New Responsibility

The Treaty of Paris, signed in 1898, gave Puerto Rico, Guam, and the Philippines to the United States and assured Cuba independence from Spain. The United States was now an imperial power, with holdings in the Caribbean and Pacific. Hawaii, the "key to the Pacific," was annexed that same year and officially became a territory of the United States in 1900.

Many people did not like the United States's new status as an empire. They believed that the United States should keep to itself and should not add territories that were outside of its borders. McKinley claimed that he did not want to leave the residents of former Spanish colonies unprotected; the United States was not so much expanding as it was looking out for those people who had been liberated from Spanish rule. Of course, there were other reasons, too.

Simply stated, the United States was expanding trade routes. A base in the Pacific could help goods and raw materials travel between the United States and Asia, and a presence in the Caribbean was strategically important in terms of the planned canal across Central America. Hawaii would connect the Pacific side of the canal with Asia.

Meanwhile, resistance to American imperialism remained a part of public life in the United States. People such as Mark Twain and Andrew Carnegie opposed American expansion. The Anti-Imperialist League had over 30,000 members. Part of the problem was in the Philippines, where, some claimed, the United States was repeating many of the wrongs the Spanish had committed in Cuba.

Not everyone was happy with McKinley expanding the president's powers and the nation's borders. Back in early 1898, as war with Spain seemed like a sure thing, the White House received seventy-three

In his campaign for the presidency, William McKinley promised Americans "Prosperity at Home, Prestige Abroad."

death threats on McKinley's life. Still, McKinley did well in the election of 1900, defeating William Jennings Bryan by more votes than he had four years earlier. The general public was happy with their president and with the result of the war. McKinley was inaugurated for his second term in 1901, and he embarked on a tour of the western states—a tour that was to end at the Pan-American Exposition in Buffalo, New York.

Leon Czolgosz, Assassin

W as Leon Czolgosz deranged? He was ruled sane after his capture, and the courts prosecuted him as sane, but later studies threw that decision into doubt.

Deranged Anarchist?

As early as 1901, doctors implied that Leon Czolgosz might have been suffering from schizophrenia, a mental illness that often strikes people in their late twenties. Czolgosz seemed stable until he hit his mid-twenties, when he suddenly "became ill" and couldn't work anymore. After his mysterious illness, he began to act strangely.

Was he an anarchist? As was mentioned earlier, anarchism is the theory that all governments should be taken apart because they keep people from acting freely. Members of anarchist organizations denied any connection with Czolgosz. They said that he had come to them for information but that they had thought he was a spy. Even if he did not join any anarchist organizations, Czolgosz was clearly influenced by anarchist beliefs. Hence, the label "deranged anarchist" sticks, and in many ways, it is appropriate.

A Good Kid, a Good Worker; Wouldn't Kill a Fly

Leon Czolgosz was born in Detroit, Michigan, into a family of six boys and two girls. According to his father, little Leon was a healthy child, but he was very shy and didn't play with many other children. Leon was educated in the public schools of Detroit and then went to Cleveland, Ohio, in search of work.

From 1892 to 1898, Czolgosz worked in the wire mills in Newburg, outside of Cleveland. According to his brother, the days were long and tiring, and Leon complained that he had very little spare time for reading. In 1893, however, he went on strike with the other workers and was fired from his job. He reapplied in 1894, using the fake name Fred C. Neiman because his real name was on management's lists of strikers not to be hired back. (When captured after shooting McKinley, Czolgosz gave this pseudonym.)

Those who knew Czolgosz described him as calm and not one to hang around with many women. Other workers at the wire factory thought of Czolgosz as a "steady worker" and remembered him as being quiet and cheerful. He didn't fight or argue with the other workers, and he worked steadily without a break.

According to a Mrs. Dryer, who owned the saloon Czolgosz visited after work, Leon liked to sit and read the paper. He played cards occasionally, though he never got visibly angry if he lost. He never swore or used dirty language. He seemed to have trouble talking to women; he may not have had the courage to speak to them. He was careful with his money and never got drunk. And, oddly enough, while Czolgosz was in the saloon, Mrs. Dryer noted, he wouldn't even kill a fly. He used to brush them off, and sometimes if he would catch one, he would just let it go.

Breakdown

In 1898, four years after the strike, Czolgosz quit his job, claiming that he had become ill. The other workers were surprised. He said that his doctors told him to stop working. He became sullen, pale, and withdrawn. He moved to the family farm, which his family had pooled their money to buy. There he did not do any heavy work unless he absolutely had to. Czolgosz spent most of his time alone, reading, sleeping, or hunting rabbits.

Czolgosz's brothers and a sister-in-law said that he spent most of his time reading or sleeping under trees, and that near the end of his stay, he would not eat anything at the dinner table. Instead, he would eat bread, milk, and a little cake—all of which he took upstairs to eat alone in his room. He let his clothes disintegrate into rags and he did not seem to care about his appearance.

In the very last months of his stay on the farm, Czolgosz's eating habits became even more peculiar. Just after the cows had been milked, he would put his milk in the cellar. He would catch fish in a pond and keep them until his stepmother was out of the house, at which time he would cook them himself. If she came home, or if strangers arrived, he would throw the fish away. Czolgosz seemed to be getting more and more paranoid—afraid that people were after him—and antisocial, avoiding people whenever he could.

By 1901, Czolgosz wanted to leave. He wanted his share of the money he had put into the family farm so he could go back to the city. He told his family that he had been attending meetings in the city, but no one knew what kind of meetings he'd been going to.

Anarchy in the U.S.A.

At this time, the presidency was more powerful than ever, and the country was spreading its influence beyond its borders. However, many people weren't happy with how things were. Workers and immigrants had seen firsthand how those with too much power mistreated them. Americans (many of whom were newly arrived immigrants) were involved in workers' unions. (A union is formed when workers band together to improve their working conditions. If the conditions do not improve, the entire union can strike, refusing to work until things change. In this way, the workers can exercise some power over bosses.) Some politically minded people embraced anarchy, which opposes the idea of having leaders at all.

Emma Goldman

At the turn of the century, Emma Goldman was the most famous American anarchist. She was born in Russia in 1869 and immigrated to the United States in 1885, when she was fifteen years old. She lectured about anarchist thought and other "radical" ideas, some of which do not seem so radical today—women's equality, availability of birth control, workers' rights, and individual liberty.

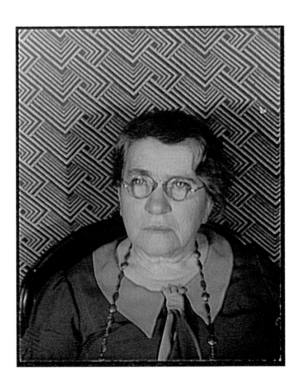

The United States eventually deported Emma Goldman because of her involvement in the anarchist movement.

Goldman moved to New York City from Rochester, New York, in 1889. In New York City, she worked in a clothing factory. Goldman had grown up with money and wanted to see the "want and suffering of the world" in person. Her experience working in clothing sweatshops increased her desire to spread her revolutionary ideas. She saw firsthand the awful conditions the workers had to endure. The workers had formed a union, called the Waist and Shirtmaker Girls' Union. When the union went on strike to try to improve their conditions, Goldman was one of the head organizers. As for being a leader of any strike or movement, Emma Goldman had this to say: "I have never been an Anarchist leader. I cannot afford it. A leader must be a diplomat. I am not a diplomat. A leader of a party makes concessions to his party, for the sake of holding his power . . . I can't do all that. I am an Anarchist because I love individual freedom and I will not surrender that freedom."

As for violence, Emma Goldman said, "I have never advocated violence, but neither do I condemn the anarchist who resorts to it. I look behind him for the conditions that made him possible, and my horror turns to pity."

Gripped by Anarchist Messages

When Czolgosz was caught, he said that what inspired him to action was a speech on anarchy that Emma Goldman gave in Cleveland in May 1901. Czolgosz claimed that her "doctrine that all rulers should be exterminated was what set [him] to thinking." As this quotation demonstrates, Czolgosz had developed a passion for anarchy's messages, without necessarily understanding them very deeply.

Emma Goldman stands on a car to speak at Union Square in New York City on May 21, 1916. It was a pivotal moment for American workers: She introduced the concept of organized labor to help protect them from the abuses of management and corporate titans.

The Lure of a Secret Society

Czolgosz contacted Emil Shilling, a well-known Cleveland anarchist, to see if he could find out more about joining up with the movement. He told Shilling that he had been a socialist but had split from them a year before. (Socialists believe that the community as a whole should own and control everything as a group. They often form unions and fight for workers' rights.) Shilling gave Czolgosz some anarchist literature and invited him over for dinner. Czolgosz kept asking about secret meetings and whether or not the anarchists had

any plans. Meanwhile, Shilling could tell that Czolgosz knew very little about anarchism except that it was antigovernment. Czolgosz's lack of knowledge about the movement made Shilling suspicious.

Czolgosz visited Shilling several times over the next months, often asking to be introduced to Emma Goldman. Czolgosz seemed gripped by the idea of the anarchists having a secret society and claimed that he wanted to do something about the poor treatment of workers. The poor treatment of workers was, and still is, a genuine problem. Many people, especially immigrants, were being forced to work extremely long hours under horrible conditions for very little money. Czolgosz got riled up about the idea of antigovernment action, but he did not seem to explain how this would help the workers. He acted so suspiciously that Shilling and other anarchists decided that he must have been a spy.

As a matter of fact, a man named E. J. Isaak published a notice in the September 1, 1901, issue of *Free Society*, an anarchist newspaper, warning everyone about the presence of a spy. The description appears to match Czolgosz, and this piece of evidence was later presented to the police to show that the anarchist movement, including Goldman, Shilling, and Isaak, wanted nothing to do with Leon Czolgosz.

Czolgosz himself seemed confused as to whether or not he was a socialist or an anarchist. There is no question that he was deeply influenced by Emma

Goldman's lectures, and that the focus of his anger and frustration was the United States government that was formed according to McKinley. He was troubled by the "outrages committed by the American government in the Philippine Islands," and said that they didn't "harmonize with the teachings in our public schools about the flag."

It is not known exactly when Czolgosz decided to kill the president, but in his confession, he said that he "planned [on] killing the president three or four days after [he] came to Buffalo." At that time, he said that he got the idea from a passage in the *Free Society*.

Was Czolgosz Mentally Ill?

Although the court ruled that Czolgosz was sane, other studies, such as one by Walter Channing in 1902, question that earlier decision. Czolgosz's family history shows that one of his aunts was insane, and insanity is often hereditary. This was not taken into account at his trial because family history was not gathered. In addition, Czolgosz's seeming mental breakdown—his sudden change from being an industrious, hardworking, quiet young man to someone who was self-absorbed, restless, and prone to fanaticism—in his mid-twenties means that he might have been schizophrenic. At the very least, Czolgosz was deranged enough to shoot the president.

The World in Mourning and Justice Served

After the shooting, McKinley hung on to life for eight days. The nation waited eagerly for news from Buffalo. At first, the news was encouraging. The surgeries had been successful; McKinley seemed to be recovering well. But then, without warning, he took a turn for the worse in the early morning hours of September 13 and died twenty-four hours later of a gangrenous infection in his stomach and pancreas.

News of McKinley's Death Shocks the Nation

In the period between the shooting and McKinley's death, everyone was concerned about how to break the news of McKinley's condition to Mrs. McKinley. She was very sensitive and delicate, and the doctors worried that bad news might worsen her various medical conditions. After all, for most of the past

years, she had depended on William McKinley for her well-being. Some hours before he died, the president asked for Mrs. McKinley. In those evening hours, they spent time alone together, and she understood that he was going to die that night.

People around the world were waiting for news about McKinley's condition. They had heard that he was recovering well from surgery after the shooting. When they heard that the president of the United States had died, messages of condolence flooded the Executive Mansion. Flags flew at half-staff in cities all over the world.

Theodore Roosevelt became popular with the Rough Riders in the Spanish-American War and became the president after McKinley's death.

Theodore Roosevelt Becomes President

McKinley's sudden turn for the worse came as a surprise to everyone who had been following his recovery from the shooting. As a matter of fact, Vice President Theodore Roosevelt, confident that McKinley would recover, wasn't near any major cities when the president died.

He was out in the Adirondack Mountains, enjoying the wilderness. He was found by a messenger and arrived in Buffalo the next day.

On September 14, 1901, Roosevelt was sworn in as the twenty-sixth president of the United States. At age forty-two, he was the youngest man ever to have that position. His first proclamation as president was a tribute to McKinley, in which he declared September 19, 1901, the day on which the president would be buried, as a national day of mourning and prayer.

Three Funerals

There were three separate funerals for McKinley. The first funeral—held in the Milburn house in Buffalo, where he had died—was simple and private. McKinley's body was brought by train to Washington, D.C., for the second funeral. The funeral train was draped in black, and the casket holding McKinley's body was elevated in the observation car so that the public could see it. The second funeral began with a private viewing at the Executive Mansion (Teddy Roosevelt renamed it the White House in 1901 by executive order) for friends and family only. Mrs. McKinley spent much of the night sitting by the casket, and she was so devastated that the doctors decided she shouldn't go to the public ceremony the next day.

Many people attended President McKinley's funeral. His numerous friends and associates filled the church with flowers.

The public ceremony, attended by thousands despite rain in Washington, included a funeral sermon, in which Bishop Edward G. Andrews of the Methodist Episcopal Church characterized McKinley as a man of "calm and equitable temperament" and "of incorruptible integrity." The third funeral was in Canton, Ohio, the president's hometown and the eventual site of the McKinley Memorial. He was buried there on September 18, 1901, in Westlawn Cemetery.

The World Reacts to the News

When news of McKinley's death reached England by telegraph, thousands of people—English and American—attended church services in McKinley's honor. The London newspapers were printed with black borders around them, and many people hung black crepe paper in their windows to express their sympathy. The king of England declared that the court should wear mourning clothes for a week. Religious and state services were also held in Canada, Mexico, Cuba, Puerto Rico, Germany, France, and many other places, including India and China.

12432—The Funeral of President McKinley—Crowd Waiting for a Last Look at the Beloved Remains, Washington, D. C., U. S. A.

Throngs of mourners in Washington, D.C., pay their respects to President McKinley, whose body was on its way to his hometown of Canton, Ohio, for a private funeral.

Plot Suspected: Anarchists Arrested

Speeches made in the wake of McKinley's death made it clear that the public wasn't satisfied with blaming only Leon Czolgosz for taking the life of their president. Czolgosz had declared himself an anarchist, and as a result, anger against anarchists as a group quickly spread across the nation.

Right after the shooting occurred, Czolgosz claimed to be a disciple, or follower, of Emma Goldman. Immediately, police in many cities began trying to track her down. It was thought that the murder of the president might have been part of a larger conspiracy; in other words, they thought that Czolgosz might have acted on orders from a secret group that wanted to overthrow the government.

In Chicago, the police captured and arrested some anarchists, and the evidence they collected led them to St. Louis, where they found no sign of Emma Goldman. Eventually, though, they found her in Chicago and arrested her, charging her with conspiring, or planning, with other anarchists to kill President McKinley.

After a period of questioning, the anarchists were released because the police couldn't find any evidence of a plot. The anarchists had claimed that they had been suspicious of the man who called himself Neiman (Czolgosz) and that they had thought he was a spy for the police or for the government. The police believed their claim because they had produced a copy of the September 1, 1901, "spy warning" in the *Free Society*, further indicating that the anarchists had avoided associating with Czolgosz. Because of this, the authorities were forced to accept that Leon Czolgosz had acted alone.

Czolgosz: Custody and Trial

In his first interview after his arrest, conducted on
September 7 and 8, 1901, Czolgosz spoke about his
crime and why he did it:

> *I don't believe in the Republican system and I
> don't believe we should have any rulers. It is
> right to kill them. I had that idea when I shot the
> president, and that is why I was there. I planned
> killing the president three or four days after I
> came to Buffalo. Something I read in the* Free
> Society *gave me the idea. I thought it would
> be a good thing for the country to kill the
> president . . . I killed President McKinley
> because I done my duty. I don't believe in
> one man having so much service, and
> another man should have none.*

After this initial interview, Czolgosz refused to
speak about the crime at all and would speak with
authorities only about other subjects.

Other than one outburst (when they told him they
were bringing in a priest to talk to him), Czolgosz was
a model prisoner. It was noted that while in custody,
Czolgosz often took his handkerchief from his pocket
and wrapped it around his right hand, as if he was
wrapping the gun in it all over again.

On Monday, September 23, 1901, Czolgosz went to trial for the murder of President McKinley. He refused to say if he wanted lawyers to represent him, so the court appointed two lawyers to plead his case. He entered a guilty plea, but his lawyers changed it to not guilty. Most of the prosecution's evidence was presented by mid-afternoon of the next day. Czolgosz's lawyers were not able to help him very much, especially because he refused to respond to their questions. There were no defense witnesses. Two psychiatrists testified to say that, judging from Czolgosz's behavior after the crime, he seemed to be sane and in good mental health. This prevented Czolgosz's lawyers from using insanity as a defense.

LESLIE'S WEEKLY
McKINLEY EXTRA

New York, September 9, 1901   PRICE 10 CENTS

LEON F. CZOLGOSZ, THE ASSASSIN.

This is a reproduction of the first photograph taken of Leon Czolgosz in jail. The photo was taken after he had assassinated McKinley in 1901.

Thomas Edison's film company reenacted the execution of Leon Czolgosz based on the description of an eyewitness. In this still from the film, Czolgosz is shown strapped into the electric chair.

After deliberations of only a half hour, the jury returned and found him guilty of first-degree murder. Two days later, the judge handed down the sentence: Czolgosz would be put to death in one month.

Czolgosz's Execution

Although he had hardly talked at all during the trial, Czolgosz wanted to make a public speech before his execution. His request was refused, so he made as much of his speech as possible while the prison guards were strapping him to the electric chair: "I shot the president because I thought it would help the working people and for the sake of the common people. I am not sorry for my crime." On October 28, 1901, Leon F. Czolgosz was executed. His body was buried in the cemetery attached to the prison, and quicklime (a corrosive chemical) and acid were poured on it to completely destroy it.

McKinley's Legacy

As a statesman, McKinley was responsible for bringing the United States to prominence as a world power and for leading America through the Spanish-American War. He also brought the nation into a new era of prosperity. He led the country into a new century and expanded the reach of American interests around the world, augmenting diplomatic channels and trade routes beyond anything previously experienced in U.S. history. Finally, he took the first steps toward planning a canal across Central America, to link the Pacific and Atlantic sea routes—a stunning example of the United States exercising its interests abroad.

How McKinley Is Remembered

More than for these achievements, however, McKinley is remembered for the personal qualities that made him a powerful leader.

He was a modest man who was very interested in people's opinions. He was curious about how Americans wanted him to lead their country. This made him a cautious leader, and one who led without showmanship. McKinley had a tremendous ability to concentrate on tasks. He was tolerant and did not hold grudges. Sometimes, this made people think that he was weak. For instance, when he was a kid, schoolmates called him "Fatty." He simply ignored them and forgave their taunts. In the end, he proved stronger than they thought. As a husband, William McKinley was admirable. He was always careful to take care of his wife, Ida, especially when she fell ill. She suffered a variety of illnesses, including phlebitis, epilepsy, and depression.

Martyrdom

McKinley's assassination turned him into a martyr (a person who has died for a cause). McKinley's life and tragic death have been commemorated in many ways. The highest mountain in the United States, Mount McKinley, is named for him. Located in Alaska's Denali National Park, the mountain was formerly called Densmore's Peak (after a prospector) by the English, Denali ("The High One") by Native Americans, and Bolshaya Gora ("Great Mountain") by the Russians. It was renamed after McKinley

Denali National Park and Preserve in Alaska features North America's highest mountain, the 20,320-foot-tall Mount McKinley. Many people refer to the mountain as Denali, it's traditional Native American name.

while he was still alive, in 1897, but one wonders if the name would have stuck had he not become a martyr.

Even a hundred years after his death, McKinley's birthday is still celebrated. He was born on January 29, 1843, and even now, every January 29 is known as Carnation Day. Members of the United States Congress receive a red carnation, similar to McKinley's "good luck" scarlet carnation, in memory of the president. McKinley is also commemorated on American money; his portrait is on the $500 bill. Hence, even as the assassin and his cause have slid into historical obscurity, the man he assassinated became even more prominent and popular than ever before.

Vice President Roosevelt Takes Over: McKinley's Dream Comes True

It is ironic that Czolgosz's "plan" to prevent McKinley from further invoking his power as president actually resulted in the executive branch being transformed into an even more powerful entity.

McKinley's successor was Vice President Theodore Roosevelt, who had distinguished himself as a military commander in the Spanish-American War. Roosevelt, the biggest hero to come out of the Spanish-American War, lead a division called the Rough Riders to a victory in the Battle of Santiago. Once Roosevelt became president, he expanded presidential powers. As he said in a letter to a British historian, "I believe in a strong executive; I believe in power." Can you imagine a statement more opposed to Czolgosz's aims?

Teddy Roosevelt is depicted in a 1905 political cartoon about the Panama Canal as "the man who can make dirt fly."

When he was vice president, Roosevelt was unhappy with the lack of power he had in his job. Perhaps you've heard the expression "Speak softly and carry a big stick." This was Roosevelt's motto, and it reflected his way of doing things around the world. When McKinley died, Roosevelt pledged to continue McKinley's policies, and he did so in his own way. Among other things, he helped make true McKinley's dream of a Central American canal by helping Panama to separate from Colombia so that a secure canal zone could be built.

McKinley's Legacy

Roosevelt became a more famous president than McKinley, in part because of his strong personality and big ideas. For a long time, historians gave him much credit for the things that McKinley started, like the expansion of the president's powers and the expansion of American interests in the world at large. However, as historians have had time to reassess the past, they now recognize William McKinley as the first modern president, the one who, for better or worse, took some of the first steps toward making America's highest office what it is today. That is McKinley's greatest legacy.

McKinley and World Politics

March 1897
McKinley is sworn in as president, and Garret A. Hobart is sworn in as vice president.

August 1897
While celebrating Uruguay's Independence Day, President Juan Idiarte Borda of Uruguay is shot and killed by an assassin.

September 1897
Failed attempt to assassinate General Porfirio Diaz of Mexico.

November 1897
An attack on the Brazilian president kills two.

January 1898
The battleship USS *Maine* arrives in Havana harbor, Cuba.

February 1898
The *Maine* explodes in Havana harbor.

March 1898
McKinley asks for and receives $50 million to be used at his discretion for "national defense."

April 1898
A bomb sent to President McKinley is disarmed.

The United States declares war against Spain.

May 1898
The Spanish fleet at Manila, Philippines, is destroyed by Commodore George Dewey and the American fleet.

July 1898
El Caney and San Juan, Cuba, are taken by American troops. The Spanish fleet in Cuba is destroyed while trying to escape.

August 1898

Peace is proclaimed and an armistice is signed between the United States and Spain.

October 1898

The United States takes possession of Puerto Rico, the Philippines, and Guam.

December 1898

The Treaty of Paris formally ends the war between Spain and the United States.

November 1899

Vice President Hobart dies and is replaced by war hero Theodore Roosevelt.

March 1900

McKinley signs the Gold Standard Act.

July 1900

King Humbert of Italy is assassinated by an anarchist named Gaetano Bresci from Paterson, New Jersey.

November 1900

McKinley wins reelection with Roosevelt as his running mate.

January 1901

Queen Victoria of England dies.

April 1901

The president and first lady, Ida McKinley, embark on an extended tour of the United States, reaching San Francisco in May. The tour is stopped because of Mrs. McKinley's illness. A planned visit to the Pan-American Exposition in Buffalo, New York, is postponed until September.

September 1901

President McKinley is assassinated at the Pan-American Exposition by Leon Czolgosz.

Glossary

anarchism   Belief that society should have no government or leaders; it also advocates a society based on the voluntary cooperation of individuals and groups.

annex   Attach or incorporate into something.

epilepsy   Condition of convulsions caused by disturbed electrical impulses in the brain.

imperialism   Belief that a country should acquire colonies and dependencies to extend its influence around the world.

intervene   To come between two parties.

phlebitis   Inflammation, or swelling, of a vein.

radical   Unusual or untraditional.

schizophrenia   Mental illness in which the relations between thoughts, feelings, and actions have broken down; often includes withdrawal from social activity and delusional thinking.

socialism   Belief that the community as a whole should own and control everything as a group.

territory   Area or region (often partly self-governing) that is run by an external government.

For More Information

McKinley Memorial Library and Museum
46 North Main Street
Niles, OH 44446
(330) 652-1704
e-mail: mckinley@oplin.lib.oh.us
Web site: http://www.mckinley.lib.oh.us

McKinley Museum and National Memorial
800 McKinley Monument Drive NW
Canton, OH 44708
(330) 455-7043
Web site: http://mckinleymuseum.org

Web Sites

Assassination of President McKinley
http://dwardmac.pitzer.edu/Anarchist_Archives/
    critics/mckinley/graphics.html
Pictures and graphics related to the assassination, plus
    a link to the Anarchy Archives, with a wealth of
    information on anarchy, past and present.

The Assassination of President McKinley
Bibliography on Medical Aspects
http://ublib.buffalo.edu/libraries/units/hsl/history/
    mckinley.html

Collections for the National Digital Library
http://rs6.loc.gov/ammem/amhome.html

The Era of William McKinley
http://www.cohums.ohio-state.edu/history/projects/
    McKinley
Information and pictures of McKinley.

The Internet Public Library Presidents of the
    United States
http://www.ipl.org/ref/POTUS/wmckinley.html

The McKinley Museum and National Memorial
http://mckinleymuseum.org
Great starting point, with resources for kids and adults.

The Spanish American War Centennial Website
http://www.spanamwar.com
Spanish-American War information.

The White House Online
http://www.whitehouse.gov

For Further Reading

Armstrong, William H. *Major McKinley: William McKinley and the Civil War*. Kent, OH: Kent State University Press, 2000.

Higgins, Eva. *William McKinley: An Inspiring Biography*. Canton, OH: Daring Pub. Group, 1989.

Johns, A. Wesley. *The Man Who Shot McKinley*. New York: A. S. Barnes and Company, 1970.

McElroy, Richard L. *William McKinley and Our America: A Pictorial History*. Canton, OH: Stark County Historical Society, 1996.

Musicant, Ivan. *Empire by Default: The Spanish-American War and the Dawn of the American Century*. New York: Henry Holt and Company, 1998.

Potter, John Mason. *Plots Against Presidents*. New York: Astor-Honor, Inc., 1968.

Index

Index

About the Author

Antoine Wilson lives in Marina Del Rey, California.

Photo Credits

Cover portrait © Frances Benjamin Johnston/The Library of Congress, Prints & Photographs Division; pp. 1, 8, 13, 17, 20, 25, 39, 43, 45, 54 © Bettmann/Corbis; p. 4 © Lee Snider/Corbis; p. 10 © Rykoff Collection/ Corbis; pp. 14, 23 © Hulton/Archive; pp. 15, 32, 37, 46, 49 © The Library of Congress, Prints & Photographs Division; p. 26 © Culver Pictures; p. 30 © Underwood & Underwood/Corbis; p. 50 © Thomas A. Edison/Camera: Edwin S. Porter/Library of Congress, Prints & Photographs Division; p. 53 © Kennan Ward/Corbis.

Series Design and Layout

Les Kanturek